Funnybunch

*In memory of
John Burnhams,
excellent teacher at
Peckhurst Junior School, Bromley:
the boy done good.*

Other anthologies by Kit Wright

POEMS FOR OVER 10-YEAR-OLDS
POEMS FOR 9-YEAR-OLDS AND UNDER

Some collections by Kit Wright

CAT AMONG THE PIGEONS
HOT DOG AND OTHER POEMS

Funnybunch

A New Puffin Book of Funny Verse

Selected by Kit Wright

Illustrated by Michael Foreman

VIKING

VIKING

Published by the Penguin Group
Penguin Books Ltd, 27 Wrights Lane, London w8 5TZ, England
Penguin Books USA Inc., 375 Hudson Street, New York, New York 10014, USA
Penguin Books Australia Ltd, Ringwood, Victoria, Australia
Penguin Books Canada Ltd, 10 Alcorn Avenue, Toronto, Ontario, Canada M4V 3B2
Penguin Books (NZ) Ltd, 182–190 Wairau Road, Auckland 10, New Zealand

Penguin Books Ltd, Registered Offices: Harmondsworth, Middlesex, England

First published 1993
10 9 8 7 6 5 4 3 2 1
First edition

This selection copyright © Kit Wright, 1993
Illustrations copyright © Michael Foreman, 1993

The Acknowledgements on pp. 159–160 constitute an extension of this copyright page.

The moral right of the author and illustrator has been asserted

All rights reserved. Without limiting the rights under copyright reserved above, no part of this publication may be reproduced, stored in or introduced into a retrieval system, or transmitted, in any form or by any means (electronic, mechanical, photocopying, recording or otherwise), without the prior written permission of both the copyright owner and the above publisher of this book

Typeset by Datix International Limited, Bungay, Suffolk
Filmset in Monophoto Sabon
Printed in England by Clays Ltd, St Ives plc

A CIP catalogue record for this book is available from the British Library

ISBN 0-670-82959-5

Contents

INTRODUCTION	9
Ladies and Gentlemen *Anon.*	9
ANIMALS ARE BEASTS!	11
I Had a Haddock *Patrick Barrington*	13
Don't Call Alligator Long-Mouth Till You Cross River *John Agard*	16
Rover *Adrian Henri*	16
The Gnu *Michael Flanders*	18
Fish Fingers *Robin Klein*	19
My Dog *Max Fatchen*	20
My Rabbit *June Crebbin*	21
From the Horse's Mouth *Raymond Wilson*	22
Nibbler *Mairaed O'Grady*	23
Moby Duck *Terry Jones*	24
The Rooster *Anon.*	26
The Frog *Anon.*	27
Up in the Air *Mary Macdonald*	28
Mosquito *N. Bodecker*	28
The Unicorn *Finola Akister*	29
Hickory, Dickory, Dock *Anon.*	29
The Hippopotamus *Michael Flanders*	30
Missing Persons *Colin Thiele*	32
RUM RELATIVES AND ODD ANCESTORS	33
Hot Food *Michael Rosen*	35
Ben *Colin West*	37
Tall Tales *Valerie Bloom*	38
Zeroing In *Diane Dawber*	39
Lost and Found *Richard Edwards*	40
With the Drier Switched to High *Charles Wright*	41
Sammy *Willy Russell*	42

WITH LOVE (AND WITHOUT)   45

Love Poem   *Anon. (completed by Roland de Vere, Lord Tryermane)*   47
Not a Love Poem   *Anon.*   48
Two Lovers Stood on Sydney Bridge   *Anon.*   48
Remarked a Young Fellow Called Hammer   *Anon.*   49
There Was a Young Fellow Called Tate   *Anon.*   49
The Frozen Logger   *Anon.*   50
The Girl I Did Not Marry   *Vernon Scannell*   52
Sisters   *Anon.*   54
Don't Hit Your Sister   *Lesley Miranda*   54
Miss Murgatroyd   *Colin West*   55
Hurrah!   *Martin Doyle*   56
I Once Thought a Lot of a Friend   *Anon.*   56
Mashed Potato/Love Poem   *Sidney Hoddes*   57
Pain   *Martin Doyle*   57
My Dear Mungo   *Matthew Sweeney*   58
Goodbye   *John Mole*   60
Prayer to St Grobianus   *Roger McGough*   62
Horrible Things   *Roy Fuller*   63
Mr Miss   *Anon.*   64

CURIOUS OCCUPATIONS   65

from I was a Bustle-maker Once, Girls   *Patrick Barrington*   67
Raising Frogs for Profit   *Anon.*   68
The Wizard Said: *Richard Edwards*   69
The Fabulous Wizard of Oz   *Anon.*   70
Potato Clock   *Roger McGough*   70
Carelessness   *Harry Graham*   72
Playing With Words   *Michael Rosen*   73
A Brother, When Asked by the Prior   *Anon.*   74
There Was a Young Bard of Japan   *Anon.*   75
Lim   *Gerard Benson*   76
Shopping   *Audrey Gorle*   77

Rules *Karla Kuskin*	78
Bebe Belinda and Carl Columbus *Adrian Mitchell*	79
Down-hearted *Janeen Brian*	80
Control Calling *Max Fatchen*	81
The Entry of the Leprechauny Man into Drumloon *Gerard Benson*	82
The Tractors *Jonathan Croall*	84
The Eye *Spike Milligan*	86
Improvement *Michael Dugan*	87
Mr Lott's Allotment *Colin West*	87
I Beavered Away All the Morning *Finola Akister*	88
In an Old French Town *Carl Sandburg*	89
The McGoos *Michael Comyns*	90
Vacancies in Eden *Catherine Benson*	92
The Experts *Terry Jones*	94

SCAMS AND SCRAPES AND SCANDALS IN SCHOOL 97

The Painting Lesson *Trevor Harvey*	99
Gust Becos I Cud Not Spel *Brian Patten*	100
So I'm Proud *Jean Little*	101
Season's Greetings *Mick Gowar*	102
The Gerbil's Funeral *June Crebbin*	104
Kite *June Crebbin*	106
What Happened to Miss Frugle *Brian Patten*	107

OODLES OF NOODLES AND LASHINGS OF NOSH 109

The Battle-hymn of the Ice-cream Connoisseur *Adrian Mitchell*	111
A Cold Snack *Richard Edwards*	112
Peas and Cues *Roger McGough*	114
Auntie Meg's Cookery Book *Vernon Scannell*	115
Giving Potatoes *Adrian Mitchell*	118
Garbage Delight *Dennis Lee*	120

Things Have Changed Martin Doyle	122
Seasickness Colin Thiele	122
Dinner-time Rhyme June Crebbin	123
Don't Leave the Spoon in the Syrup N. Bodecker	124
Official Notice Adrian Mitchell	124

OF MISFITS AND MISFORTUNES — 125

More Work for the Undertaker Fred W. Leigh	127
Someone's Fear Martin Doyle	130
An Evening in November Anon.	130
The Secret Drawer Richard Edwards	131
Wobble-dee-woo Colin West	132
Cholmondeley Mick Gowar	134
Well-wishers Angela Sidey	136
Trying to Thank the Begonia Daisy Cheyne	136
The Cat and the Pig Gerard Benson	137
There Was a Young Lady of Spain Anon.	139
The Lord Said Unto Moses Anon.	139
All's Well That Ends Roger McGough	140
Success At Last Raymond Wilson	141

QUERIES AND THEORIES — 143

We All Know That Bicycle Marianne Chipperfield	145
A Query Richard Edwards	146
A Wasp on a Nettle Said: 'Coo!' Frank Richards	146
Logic Michael Rosen	147
Toe-tally Charles Wright	148
Why Did the Children Carl Sandburg	149
Glasses Sue Cowling	150
He's on About a Parrot Now Martin Doyle	151
'Which Way to the Post Office, Boy?' Carl Sandburg	152

Index of Authors	153
Index of First Lines	155
Acknowledgements	159

INTRODUCTION

Ladies and Gentlemen

Ladies and gentlemen,
I come before you to stand behind you,
To tell you something I know nothing about.
On Monday, which is Good Friday,
There will be a mothers' meeting for fathers only.
Admission is free,
You pay at the door.
Bring your own seats,
We'll sit on the floor.

Anon

Now read on . . .

ANIMALS ARE BEASTS!

I Had a Haddock

        I had a haddock,
        A young he-haddock;
His mother was from Harwich and his sire was Dutch.
        I loved that haddock,
        He was indeed a haddock!
        I never knew a haddock
           That I loved so much.

        I had a haddock;
        I kept him in the paddock –
I thought he might mistake it for the wide green sea.
        But, oh, my paddock
        Proved utterly inadequ-
        ate even for a haddock
           As obtuse as he.

I had a haddock;
I called him Major Craddock,
After Major Craddock of 'The Myrtles', Kew.
My poor haddock
Was more like Major Craddock
Than any other haddock
That I ever knew.

I took my haddock
To call on Major Craddock;
I thought it would amuse him, and the two might chat;
But Major Craddock
Objected to my haddock;
He didn't like a haddock
With a face like that.

I had a haddock;
I kept him in the paddock;
I used to see him gasping in the noonday sun.
Ah, poor haddock!
It was indeed a sad oc-
cupation for a haddock
With a sense of fun.

To help my haddock
I tried to flood the paddock;
I did it with a hosepipe, but it burst one night.
When next my haddock
Proceeded to the paddock
He fell into the water
And was drowned outright.

> I had a haddock,
> A single-hearted haddock;
> I loved my haddock as I loved my life;
> But I lost my haddock –
> I lost him in the paddock;
> And I mourned my haddock
> As I would my wife.
>
> I had a haddock;
> I also had a paddock;
> But nothing is enduring in this vale of woes.
> I lost my haddock,
> I spoilt my pretty paddock,
> I vexed Major Craddock
> And I burst my hose.

Patrick Barrington

Don't Call Alligator Long-Mouth Till You Cross River

Call alligator long-mouth
call alligator saw-mouth
call alligator pushy-mouth
call alligator scissors-mouth
call alligator raggedy-mouth
call alligator bumpy-bum
call alligator all dem rude word
but better wait
                till you cross river.

John Agard

Rover

for David Ross

I have a pet oyster call Rover.
He lives in the bathroom sink
and is never any trouble:
no birdseed or tins of Kennomeat,
no cat-litter.
We don't need to take him for walks,
we don't need an oyster-flap in the back door.

He doesn't bark
or sing,
just lies in the sink
and never says a thing.
Sometimes,
when he feels irritable,
he grits his teeth
and produces a little pearl.

At night,
we tuck him up snug in his oyster-bed
until the bathroom tide comes in
in the morning.

Sometimes
I look at Rover and say
'The world's your lobster,
Rover', I say.

Adrian Henri

The Gnu

A year ago last Thursday I was strolling in the zoo
When I met a man who thought he knew the lot;
He was laying down the law about the habits of
    Baboons
And the number of quills a Porcupine has got.
I asked him: 'What's that creature there?'
              He answered:
              'H'it's a H'elk.'
I might have gone on thinking that was true,
If the animal in question hadn't put the chap to shame
And remarked: 'I h'ain't a H'elk. I'm a G-nu!

   I'm a G-nu, I'm a G-nu,
   The g-nicest work of g-nature in the zoo!
   I'm a G-nu, how do you do?
   You really ought to k-now w-ho's w-ho.
   I'm a G-nu, spelt G.N.U.,
   I'm g-not a Camel or a Kangaroo,
   So let me introduce,
   I'm g-neither Man nor Moose,
   Oh, g-no, g-no, g-no, I'm a G-nu!'

I had taken furnished lodgings down at Rustington-on-
    Sea
(Whence I travelled on to Ashton-under-Lyme)
And the second night I stayed there, I was wakened
    from a dream
Which I'll tell you all about some other time.

Among the hunting trophies on the wall above my
   bed,
Stuffed and mounted, was a face I thought I knew.
A Bison? An Okapi? Could it be . . . A Hartebeest?
Then I seemed to hear a voice: 'I'm a G-nu!

   I'm a G-nu, a g-nother G-nu,
   I wish I could g-nash my teeth at you!
   I'm a G-nu, how do you do?
   You really ought to k-now w-ho's w-ho.
   I'm a G-nu, spelt G.N.U.,
   Call me Bison or Okapi and I'll sue!
   G-nor am I in the least
   Like that dreadful Hartebeest,
   Oh, g-no, g-no, g-no, I'm a G-nu!'

Michael Flanders

Fish Fingers

One, two, three, four, five –
Once I caught a fish alive!
Six, seven, eight, nine, ten –
Then I let it go again!
Why did I let it go?
Because it bit my finger so!
Why did I lose my cool?
Because it was a shark, you fool!

Robin Klein

My Dog

My dog is such a gentle soul,
Although he's big it's true.
He brings the paper in his mouth,
He brings the postman too.

Max Fatchen

My Rabbit

When my rabbit
is out in his run,

he digs up the ground
like a dog,

washes himself
like a squirrel,

sits on his back legs
like a kangaroo

leaps and twirls
like an acrobat,

but

when he eats a cabbage leaf,
as is his daily habit,
he delicately nibbles it
EXACTLY like a rabbit!

June Crebbin

From the Horse's Mouth

It was dusk as I strolled down a country lane
When a voice from nearby spoke plain as plain:

Did you know I won the Derby in seventy-three?
Yet when I turned round there was no one to see!

The fields stretched empty as the shadowy air
But for one old horse that was grazing there.

So on I walked down the darkening lane
When the same voice spoke, and said over again:

Did you know I won the Derby in seventy-three?
And when I looked, that horse was following me!

So I took to my heels, like a shot from a gun –
Three desperate miles to the Rising Sun.

I'd no breath to speak with, as I fell through the door,
But they helped me as if they'd seen all this before.

'You've no need to explain,' the landlord said
As he drew me a pint, and shook his grey head.

'That old horse tells more lies than have ever been
   reckoned.
It was seventy-*two*, and the beast came *second*!'

Raymond Wilson

Nibbler

Nibbler, our gerbil, died today.
Dead in his red plastic cage he lay,
His food uneaten, his wheel untrod,
I hope he'll be happy with Budgie and God.

Mairaed O'Grady

Moby Duck

Moby Duck was the terror of the river.
He could sink a punt with his mighty beak.
Moby Duck had some trouble with his liver,
And was in a filthy temper almost all the week.

Men would come to see if they could tame him,
But they had no luck and he gave 'em hell,
And I must say I don't think that you can blame him
Cause he didn't like 'em coming and he wasn't very well.

Moby Duck was the terror of the river.
He was feared by cats and dogs and geese.
Just to hear his name made the cattle go a-quiver,
And he wasn't in the good books of the local police.

He grew so big – when he got into the water –
There just was no room for another living thing.
The otters said he ate more fish than he ought to,
And he stunned wild bulls with a single wing!

Well in the end, they decided to get rid of him,
And towed that duck to the open sea.
He was quacking and complaining about everything
   they did to him,
But they got him to the ocean and they set him free.

Moby Duck didn't even stop to ponder,
He just gave a quack and he shook his tail,
And they heard him yell, as he disappeared out
   yonder:
'If you don't want me to be a duck – I'll be a whale!'

Terry Jones

The Rooster

I sometimes think I'd rather crow
And be a rooster than to roost
And be a crow. But I dunno.

A rooster he can roost also,
Which don't seem fair when crows can't crow.
Which may help some. Still I dunno.

Crows should be glad of one thing though;
Nobody thinks of eating crow,
While roosters they are good enough
For anyone unless they're tough.

There's lots of tough old roosters though.
And anyway a crow can't crow.
So mebbe roosters stand more show.
It looks that way. But I dunno.

Anon.

The Frog

What a wonderful bird the frog are –
When he sit, he stand almost;
When he hop, he fly almost.
He ain't got no sense hardly;
He ain't got no tail hardly either.
When he sit, he sit on what he ain't got –
almost.

Anon.

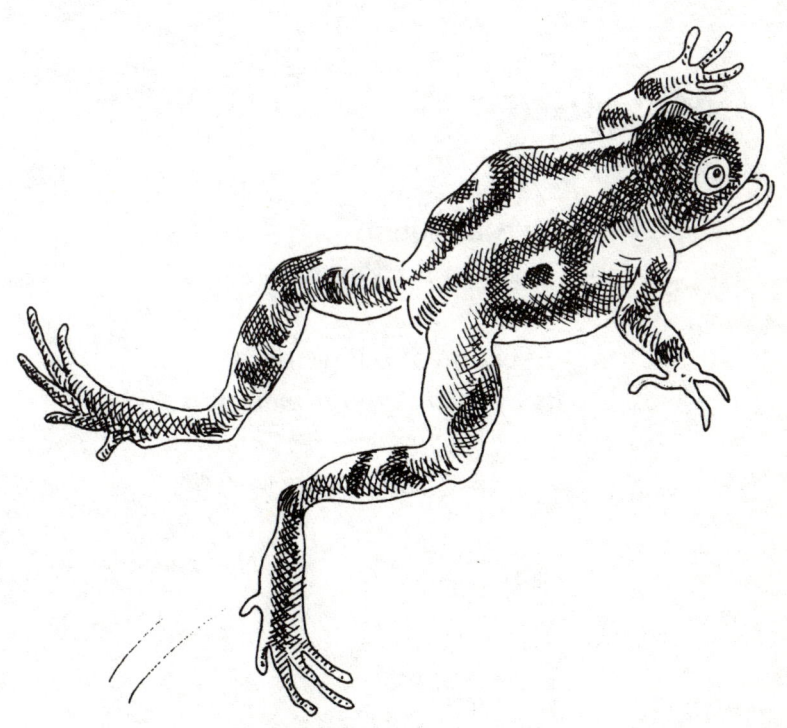

Up in the Air

Pussy cat, pussy cat, where have you been?
I've been to the airport at Tullamarine.
Pussy cat, pussy cat, what did you there?
I frightened a jumbo jet into the air.

Mary Macdonald

Mosquito

A mosquito
From Buckingham Palace
to its Maker
claimed to have been:
*By Special Appointment Purveyor
of Mosquito Bites
to the Queen.*

N. Bodecker

The Unicorn

The unicorn had one big horn
In the middle of his head.
It's doubtful if he ever lived,
And if he did, he's dead.

Finola Akister

Hickory, Dickory, Dock

Hickory, dickory, dock,
Two mice ran up the clock.
The clock struck one,
And the other one got away.

Anon.

The Hippopotamus

A bold Hippopotamus was standing one day
On the banks of the cool Shalimar.
He gazed at the bottom as it peacefully lay
By the light of the evening star.
Away on a hilltop sat combing her hair
His fair Hippopotamine maid;
The Hippopotamus was no ignoramus
And sang her this sweet serenade:

>Mud, mud, glorious mud,
>Nothing quite like it for cooling the blood!
>So follow me, follow,
>Down to the hollow
>And there let us wallow
>In glorious mud!

The fair Hippopotama he aimed to entice
From her seat on that hilltop above,
As she hadn't got a ma to give her advice,
Came tiptoeing down to her love.
Like thunder the forest re-echoed the sound
Of the song that they sang as they met.
His inamorata adjusted her garter
And lifted her voice in duet:

> Mud, mud, glorious mud,
> Nothing quite like it for cooling the blood!
> So follow me, follow,
> Down to the hollow
> And there let us wallow
> In glorious mud!

Now more Hippopotami began to convene
On the banks of that river so wide.
I wonder now what am I to say of the scene
That ensued by the Shalimar side?
They dived all at once with an ear-splitting splosh
Then rose to the surface again,
A regular army of Hippopotami
All singing this haunting refrain:

> Mud, mud, glorious mud,
> Nothing quite like it for cooling the blood!
> So follow me, follow,
> Down to the hollow
> And there let us wallow
> In glorious mud!

Michael Flanders

Missing Persons

The world's most enigmatic smile
Belongs to Crunch, our crocodile,
Who likes to lie in silent wait
Beside our shrubby garden gate.

And so detectives sometimes come
To question me and Dad and Mum
About the people, big and small,
Who seem to vanish when they call.

But nothing comes of it, of course,
Although we suffer some remorse,
For as they seek a sign or clue
Detectives seem to vanish too.

Colin Thiele

RUM RELATIVES
AND ODD ANCESTORS

Hot Food

We sit down to eat
and the potato's a bit hot
so I only put a little bit on my fork
and I blow
whooph whooph
until it's cool
just cool
then into the mouth
nice.
And there's my brother
he's doing the same
whooph whooph
into the mouth
nice.
There's my mum
she's doing the same
whooph whooph
into the mouth
nice.
But my dad.
My dad.
What does he do?
He stuffs a great big chunk of potato
into his mouth.
Then
that really does it.

His eyes pop out
he flaps his hands
he blows, he puffs, he yells
he bobs his head up and down
he spits bits of potato
all over his plate
and he turns to us and he says,
'Watch out everybody –
the potato's very hot.'

Michael Rosen

Ben

Ben's done something really bad,
He's forged a letter from his dad.
He's scrawled:

> Dear Miss,
>   Please let Ben be
> Excused this week from all P.E.
> He's got a bad cold in his chest
> And so I think it might be best
> If he throughout this week could be
> Excused from doing all P.E.
>
> I hope my ~~wright~~ writing's
>   not too bad.
>
>   Yours sincerely,
>   (signed) Ben's Dad.

Colin West

Tall Tales

I saw a silver mermaid with green and purple hair.
I saw her sitting by the river in her underwear.

No you never, you never.

I did.

I saw a rolling calf with twenty-seven toes.
I saw the smoke and fire that was coming from its
  nose.

No you never, you never.

I did.

I saw the devil dancing reggae in the bright moonlight.
I saw him sting a donkey with his tail the other night.

No you never, you never.

I did.

I saw your father busy looking at your report card.
I saw him searching for you in the house and round
  the yard.

No you never . . . you never . . . you did?

Valerie Bloom

Zeroing In

The tree down the street
   has little green apples
      that never get bigger
         never turn red.
They just drop on the ground
   get worm holes
      brown spots.
They're
   just right for stepping on
      like walking on bumpy marbles,
         or green eggs that break with a snap
           just right for gathering
              in a heap behind the hedge
                 waiting
                    for a target.
Here comes my brother.

Diane Dawber

Lost and Found

I was worrying over some homework
When my grandad walked into the room
And sat wearily down with a grunt and a frown
And a face full of sorrow and gloom.

'I've lost it, I've lost it,' he muttered,
'And it's very important to me.'
'Lost what?' I replied. 'I've forgotten,' he sighed.
'But it's something beginning with T.'

'A toffee, perhaps,' I suggested,
'Or a teapot or even your tie,
Or some toast or a thread . . .' but he shook his grey head
As a tear trickled out of one eye.

'A tuba,' I said, 'or some treacle,
Or a toggle to sew on your mac,
Or a tray or a ticket, a tree or a thicket,
A thistle, a taper, a tack.'

But Grandad looked blank. 'Well, some tweezers,
Or a theory,' I said, 'or a tooth,
Or a tap or a till or a thought or a thrill
Or your trousers, a trestle, the truth.'

'It's none of those things,' grumbled Grandad.
'A toy trumpet,' I offered, 'a towel,
Or a trout, a tureen, an antique tambourine,
A toboggan, a tortoise, a trowel . . .'

Then suddenly Grandad's scowl vanished.
'I've remembered!' he cried with a shout.
'It's my temper, you brat, so come here and take that!'
And he boxed both my ears and went out.

Richard Edwards

With the Drier Switched to High

With the drier switched to high
Father left his daughter hairless.
Mother murmured with a sigh,
'Darling, must you be so careless?'

Charles Wright

Sammy

I wish I was our Sammy
Our Sammy's nearly ten.
He's got two worms and a catapult
An' he's built a underground den.
But I'm not allowed to go in there,
I have to stay near the gate,
Cos me mam says I'm only seven,
But I'm not, I'm nearly eight!

I sometimes hate our Sammy,
He robbed me toy car y' know,
Now the wheels are missin' an' the top's broke off,
An' the bleedin' thing won' go.
An' he said when he took it, it was just like that,
But it wasn't, it went dead straight,
But y' can't say nott'n when they think y' seven
An' y' not, y' nearly eight.

I wish I was our Sammy,
Y' wanna see him spit,
Straight in y' eye from twenty yards
An' every time a hit.
He's allowed to play with matches,
And he goes to bed dead late,
And I have to go at seven,
Even though I'm nearly eight.

Y' know our Sammy,
He draws nudey women,
Without arms, or legs, or even heads
In the baths, when he goes swimmin'.
But I'm not allowed to go to the baths,
Me mam says I have to wait,
Cos I might get drowned, cos I'm only seven,
But I'm not, I'm nearly eight.

Y' know our Sammy,
Y' know what he sometimes does?
He wees straight through the letter-box
Of the house next door to us.
I tried to do it one night,
But I had to stand on a crate,
Cos I couldn't reach the letter-box
But I will by the time I'm eight.

Willy Russell

WITH LOVE
(AND WITHOUT)

Love Poem

My ❤️➳ 👙 4 U

It 👃 U R the 1

Y R U not 👂

👁 a🚪 U ☀

1st line: Anon.
Completed by
Roland De Vere, Lord Tryermane

Not a Love Poem

You are so low that, if there was a car on a bridge
and under the bridge there was a rock
and under the rock there was a stone
and under the stone there was a snail
and under the snail there was a bull ant
and under the bull ant there was a flea,
you could walk under the flea!

Anon.

Two Lovers Stood on Sydney Bridge

Two lovers stood on Sydney bridge,
Her lips were all a-quiver.
He kissed her
And her leg fell off
And floated down the river.

Anon.

Remarked a Young Fellow Called Hammer

Remarked a young fellow called Hammer,
Who had an unfortunate stammer,
    'The b . . . bane of my life
      Is my w . . . w . . . w . . . wife,
D . . . d . . . d . . . d . . . d . . . d . . . damn 'er!'

Anon.

There Was a Young Fellow Called Tate

There was a young fellow called Tate
Who dined with a girl at 8.08.
    But I'd hate to relate
    What that fellow called Tate
At his tête-à-tête ate at 8.08.

Anon.

The Frozen Logger

As I sat down one evening
In a timber town café,
A six-foot-seven waitress
To me these words did say:

'I see you are a logger
And not just a common bum,
Cos nobody but a logger stirs
His coffee with his thumb.

My lover was a logger,
There's none like him today.
If you poured whisky on it,
He'd eat a bale of hay.

He never shaved the whiskers
From off his horny hide.
He banged them in with a hammer
And bit them off inside.

My lover came to see me,
'Twas on one freezing day.
He held me in a fond embrace
That broke three vertebrae.

He kissed me when we parted
So hard it broke my jaw:
I could not speak to tell him
He forgot his mackinaw.*

I saw my lover leaving,
He sauntered through the snow,
Going bravely homeward
At forty-eight below.

The weather tried to freeze him,
It tried its level best.
At a hundred degrees below zero
He buttoned up his vest.

It froze clear through to China,
It froze to the stars above.
At a thousand degrees below zero
It froze my logger love.

And that is why this evening
To the timber town I come,
And here I wait till someone stirs
His coffee with his thumb.'

Anon.

* Coat

The Girl I Did Not Marry

When I was eighteen years of age
   I met a lovely girl;
She was so beautiful she made
   My thoughts and senses whirl.

Not only beautiful but kind,
   Intelligent as well;
Her smile was warm as India,
   Her voice a silver bell.

So gentle and so sensitive,
    She was the one for me;
We loved the same great melodies
    And peace and poetry.

In spring we wandered hand in hand
    Towards a treasured scene
To which I'd never taken her,
    Small paradise of green.

We climbed a gentle slope and then
    Walked through a little wood;
And there, below, were shining fields
    Where sheep and young lambs stood

Or danced or drifted on dry seas,
    Their bleatings frail or hoarse.
'When I see those,' my darling said,
    'I always smell mint sauce.'

Vernon Scannell

Sisters

If only I hadn't had sisters
How much more romantic I'd be
But my sisters were such little blisters
That all women are sisters to me.

Anon.

Don't Hit Your Sister

He hit me on the face, Mummy
so I hit him back

He hit me on the leg, Mummy
so I hit him back

He hit me on the back, Mummy
so I hit him back on the back

He hurlded me, Mummy
so I hurlded him back

He was the one who started it, Mummy
so I started it back.

Lesley Miranda

Miss Murgatroyd

Together down the street they go,
Beneath the one umbrella,
Miss Murgatroyd and Montague,
The brute she calls her fella.

Miss Murgatroyd loves Montague,
Wrapped in his lanky arms,
She finds within his funny face
Lie all life's hidden charms.

She finds his charming countenance
Much sweeter than most men's is.
(Perhaps she needs a pair of specs,
Or else some contact lenses.)

Together down the street they go,
And so they will until a
Spoilsport tells Miss Murgatroyd
That . . . Monty's a gorilla.

Colin West

Hurrah!

Great,
now I really feel sorted out,
I found myself muttering
as I was thumping my head
against my old friend
the cellar door
last Monday morning.

Martin Doyle

I Once Thought a Lot of a Friend

I once thought a lot of a friend,
Who turned out to be, in the end,
　　The most southerly part
　　(As I'd feared from the start)
Of a horse with a northerly trend.

Anon.

Mashed Potato/Love Poem

If I ever had to choose between you
and a third helping of mashed potato,
(whipped lightly with a fork
not whisked,
and a little pool of butter
melting in the middle . . .)

I think
I'd choose
the mashed potato.

But I'd choose you next.

Sidney Hoddes

Pain

Yesterday I thought I was someone
who I didn't particularly like,
so I socked myself in the eye.
That'll teach me.

Martin Doyle

My Dear Mungo

My dear Mungo,
it's time you went away
cleared off to Canada,
there to stay,
up in the tundra
of the frozen North –
Queen Elizabeth Islands
or worse,
where no one lives
except snowy bears
and long-teethed walruses
and snowier hares –
only up there
could I like you,

send me a snapshot
so I can see you
just as you'll be,
hair past your chin,
a glint in your eye
and ice on your grin,
mouthing your insults
and smart remarks
to leopard seals
and prowling sharks –
my dear Mungo,
head for Heathrow,
I've had it, mate,
beat it, go!

Matthew Sweeney

Goodbye

Goodbye to my blanket,
I loved how it stank! It
Was snotty and slimy
And Mum said 'It's time he
Got rid of it, burnt it.'
But I cried 'I want it,
It's cosy, it's snuggly,
Who cares if it's ugly,
Its unique aroma
Reminds me of home. Ah
Blanket, ah blanket,
You're soggy and dank yet
I love every piece of you,
All the smeared grease of you,
All the dried spittle
From when I was little
It's part of my life now,
We're like husband and wife now!'

Then I met Albert
And now he's my pal, but
He doesn't like gungy
Old blankets all spongy
And sickly and pongy.
He says it's all wrong, he
Says I should grow up,
He says I should *blow* up
My blanket, forget it;
To a well-mannered Ted it
Seems utterly nasty,
A part of my past he
Would like to see vanish
So I'm going to be mannish
And grown up and seven,
Send blanket to heaven.
I'm sorry to lose it
But I really must choose. It
Is Albert or blanket
So now I must thank it
(Dear blanket) for keeping
While waking and sleeping
Me snug, wipe the tear from my eye
And say 'Blanket, goodbye!'

John Mole

Prayer to Saint Grobianus
(The patron saint of coarse people)

Intercede for us dear saint we beseech thee
    we fuzzdutties and cullions
    dunderwhelps and trollybags
    lobcocks and loobies.

On our behalf seek divine forgiveness for
    we puzzlepates and pigsconces
    ninnyhammers and humgruffins
    gossoons and clapperdudgeons.

Have pity on we poor wretched sinners
    we blatherskites and lopdoodles
    lickspiggots and clinchpoops
    quibberdicks and quakebuttocks.

Free us from the sorrows of this world
and grant eternal happiness in the next
    we snollygosters and gundyguts
    gongoozlers and groutheads
    ploots, quoobs, lurds and swillbellies.

As it was in the beginning, is now, and ever shall be, world without end. OK?

Roger McGough

Horrible Things

'What's the horriblest thing you've seen?'
Said Nell to Jean.

'Some grey-coloured, trodden-on Plasticine;
On a plate, a left-over cold baked bean;
A cloakroom ticket numbered thirteen;
A slice of meat without any lean;
The smile of a spiteful fairy-tale queen;
A thing in the sea like a brown submarine;
A cheese fur-coated in brilliant green;
A bluebottle perched on a piece of sardine.
What's the horriblest thing *you've* seen?'
Said Jean to Nell.

'Your face, as you tell
Of all the horriblest things you've seen.'

Roy Fuller

Mr Miss

Mr   Miss
Meet Kiss
More Kisses
Mr   Mrs

Anon.

CURIOUS OCCUPATIONS

from **I Was a Bustle-maker Once, Girls**

When I was a lad of twenty
  And was working in High Street, Ken.,
I made quite a pile in a very little while –
  I was a bustle-maker then.
Then there was work in plenty,
  And I was a thriving man;
But things have decayed in the bustle-making trade
  Since the bustle-making trade began.

I built bustles with a will then;
  I built bustles with a wit;
I built bustles as a Yankee hustles,
  Simply for the love of it.
I built bustles with a skill then
  Surpassed, they say, by none;
But those were the days when bustles were the craze,
  And now those days are done.

I was a bustle-maker once, girls,
  Many, many years ago;
I put my heart in the bustle-maker's art,
  And I don't mind saying so.
I may have had the brains of a dunce, girls;
  I may have had the mind of a muff;
I may have been plain and deficient in the brain,
  But I did know a bustle-maker's stuff.

I built bustles for the slender;
    I built bustles for the stout;
I built bustles for the girls with muscles
    And bustles for the girls without.
I built bustles by the thousands once
    In the good old days of yore;
But things have decayed in the bustle-building trade,
    And I don't build bustles any more.

Patrick Barrington

Raising Frogs for Profit

Raising frogs for profit
Is a very sorry joke.
How can you make money
When so many of them croak?

Anon.

The Wizard Said:

'You find a sheltered spot that faces south . . .'
   'And then?'
'You sniff and put two fingers in your mouth . . .'
   'And then?'
'You close your eyes and roll your eye-balls round . . .'
   'And then?'
'You lift your left foot slowly off the ground . . .'
   'And then?'
'You make your palm into a kind of cup . . .'
   'And then?'
'You *very quickly* raise your right foot up . . .'
   'And then?'
'You fall over.'

Richard Edwards

The Fabulous Wizard of Oz

The fabulous Wizard of Oz
Retired from business because
    What with up-to-date science,
    To most of his clients,
He wasn't the Wizard he woz.

Anon.

Potato Clock

A potato clock, a potato clock
    Has anybody got a potato clock?
A potato clock, a potato clock
    Oh where can I find a potato clock?

I went down to London the other day
Found myself a job with a lot of pay
Carrying bricks on a building-site
From early in the morning till late at night

No one here works as hard as me
I never even break for a cup of tea
My only weakness, my only crime
Is that I can never get to work on time

A potato clock, a potato clock
    Has anybody got a potato clock?
A potato clock, a potato clock
    Oh where can I find a potato clock?

I arrived this morning half an hour late
The foreman came up in a terrible state
'You've got a good job, but you'll lose it, cock,
If you don't get up at eight o'clock.'

Up at eight o'clock, up at eight o'clock
    Has anybody got up at eight o'clock?
Up at eight o'clock, up at eight o'clock
    Oh where can I find up at eight o'clock?

Roger McGough

Carelessness

A window-cleaner in our street
Who fell (five storeys) at my feet
Impaled himself on my umbrella.
I said: 'Come, come, you careless fella!
If my umbrella had been shut
You might have landed on my nut!'

Harry Graham

Playing With Words

You can play with dice
You can play with cards
You can play with a ball
You can play with words
          words
          words
          words
          words
          words
          words
          banana
          words
          words
          words
          words
          words

Michael Rosen

A Brother, When Asked by the Prior

A Brother, when asked by the Prior,
Why he spent so much time by the fire,
    Replied, 'While you pray,
    I work here all day –
In fact I'm your chipmunk, or friar.'

Anon.

There Was a Young Bard of Japan

There was a young bard of Japan,
Whose limericks never would scan;
    When told it was so,
    He said: 'Yes, I know,
But I always try and get as many words
   into the last line as I possibly can.'

Anon.

Lim

There once was a bard of Hong Kong,
Who thought limericks were too long.

Gerard Benson

Shopping

Our neighbour, Mrs Tuckett
Went shopping in the sales.
She bought a plastic bucket
For a colony of snails,
Some purple striped pyjamas
For her second cousin's dog
And a pair of tinted glasses
For a very ancient frog.
   One hundred pairs of slippers,
      Two thousand yellow hats,
         Three million frozen kippers AND
           A dozen cricket bats.
And when on Thursday morning
She had no money left,
She stopped this silly shopping
To start a life of theft.

Audrey Gorle

Rules

Do not jump on ancient uncles.
*
Do not yell at average mice.
*
Do not wear a broom to breakfast.
*
Do not ask a snake's advice.
*
Do not bathe in chocolate pudding.
*
Do not talk to bearded bears.
*
Do not smoke cigars on sofas.
*
Do not dance on velvet chairs.
*
Do not take a whale to visit
Russell's mother's cousin's yacht.
*
And whatever else you do do
It is better you
Do not.

Karla Kuskin

Bebe Belinda and Carl Columbus
verses for Laura

There was a girl who threw bananas about
When she couldn't get bananas she threw baseball bats about
When she couldn't get baseball bats she threw big blue beehives about
And her name was Bebe, Bebe Belinda.

There was a boy who threw cuckoo clocks about
When he couldn't find cuckoo clocks he threw cucumbers about
When he couldn't find cucumbers he went crackers and threw christening cakes about
And his name was Carl, Carl Columbus.

In Hanover Terrace, that magical place,
Bebe and Carl met, face to red face.
She bust his cuckoo clock with a bunch of bananas.
In a swashbuckling sword-fight his cucumber cutlass
Carved her baseball bat to bits.
She bashed him on the bonce with her best blue beehive
But he craftily crowned her with a christening cake.

And they left it to me, old Lizzie Lush
To clean up the street with my scrubbing-brush.

Adrian Mitchell   BRIGHTON, 1981

Down-hearted

If I were Chief of all Spacemen,
I'd be known as Astra-Ten.
But Astra-Nine
Would be quite fine
And Astra-Eight would be just great.
Seven, six, five or four,
I wouldn't ever ask for more.
Astra-Three or Astra-Two,
Even Astra-One would do.
But sad to say, although I've fought,
I'm still just plain old Astra-Nought!

Janeen Brian

Control Calling

Just when I am conducting
A manoeuvre tactical
On my spaceship galactical,
Using my unidentified-object locators,
With my forward disintegrators
Whamming and shooting,
And my astro-clad officers saluting
Amid the rocketry's swirls and swishes,
My sister Kate
Cries, 'Activate!'
And I'm back on earth,
Drying dishes.

Max Fatchen

The Entry of the Leprechauny Man into Drumloon

When the
par-
tickle-u-lar-
ly
leprechauny man
made entrancement
through the noble mahoganish gates
of the metropololical city
of Drumloon
polished bands
played giggly music
in the cobblers lanes and alleys
and the washerwomen
uplifting their kirtlekilts
to above fat knees
danced boldsteppings
all up and down the city.
He
with a leprecaper
conjoined his insignificable self
to the dancing
and all aroundle the dignificent
Monument
of Mayor Augustus de Rahilly (mounted)

childerpeople, doglets, fat women and thin men
reeled, jiggied and pranked
in eccentrical cavorts and circlets.
When midnight fell
out of the crested sky
all drabs and dribs
returned out of breath to their homeplaces
leaving the town square
the stone manely rearing horse
with its obsequious rider
and also the tinkling stars
to the amazed and the partickleular appreciate
of the leprechauny man
who sang to himself
little darksoft nightsongs
until he lidded his eyes
and slept.

Gerard Benson

The Tractors

From where I   stood
I could see
s e v e n t e e n tractors
perched   on   the   hillside

And   when I looked closer   I saw that

    inside
    one
    of
    them
    there was a man
    who had his head
                      cocked
                      on
                          one
                              side

And I wondered if he was
    listening to the Test Match
    or whether he was always

        that
          way
            inclined

because his farm was

on
  the
    hill-
      side.

Jonathan Croall

The Eye

A man went to an antique shop
And there he did espy
A great historical object,
A very old glass eye.
The man said to the salesman,
'What's this, may I inquire?'
'Lord Nelson's glass eye,' said the man
'And it's looking for a buyer.'

Spike Milligan

Improvement

Old uncle Samuel, felling trees,
cut his legs off at the knees.
'I'll sew them back,' cried his daughter.
'No,' said Sam, 'I like them shorter.'

Michael Dugan

Mr Lott's Allotment

Mr Lott's allotment
Meant a lot to Mr Lott.
Now Mr Lott is missed a lot
On Mr Lott's allotment.

Colin West

I Beavered Away All the Morning

I beavered away all the morning,
I beavered the whole day through.
When you happen to be a beaver,
There's nothing much else you can do.

Finola Akister

In an Old French Town

In an old French town
the mayor ordered the people
to hang lanterns in front of their houses
which the people did
but the lanterns gave no light
so the mayor ordered they must
put candles in the lanterns
which the people did
but the candles in the lanterns gave no light
whereupon the mayor ordered
they must light the candles in the lanterns
which the people did
and thereupon there was light.

Carl Sandburg

The McGoos

On the coast of Timbuctoo
Where the fun and games are few
And the turtles seldom flap a flippant flipper

Lives Archibald McGoo
And Mrs McGoo too
And they do not welcome tourist, tramp or tripper.

They sit upon the strand
Like the lords of all the land
And it's every piece of bladderwrack and jetsam,

Oh I beg you, don't inquire
If their deckchairs are for hire
For the commonplace or mundane merely frets 'em.

Be it morning, noon or night
They like to do things right
And wear the proper dress for each occasion.

Because they're very wise
They take daily exercise
And are of a vegetarian persuasion.

Watch them walk along the pier
From the far end to the near
And back again but never see the sea.

It's because it goes away
At about this time of day
And returns at five to four in time for tea.

Michael Comyns

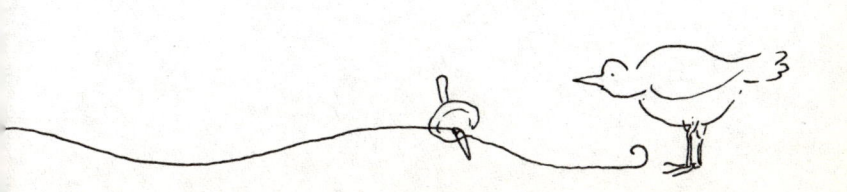

Vacancies in Eden
or
(Wanted: two gardeners m/f)

Garden of Eden?
That would be bliss,
Sheer bliss, a holiday.

I'm a maid in Heaven.
I rise before dawn,
Set the fire in the east,
Bake the morning's manna,
Fill the clouds with raindrops,
Polish the rainbow,
Wake up the breeze,
Stoke the sun,
Then I'm off duty till dusk.

Back to rake the ashes in the west,
Damp down the fire,
Set out the stars,
Hang out the moon,
Dust the moonbeams,
Finally, spread the coverlet of sleep
(Taking a corner for myself to rest and dream).

Then it's up and set the fire . . .
Day after night
Day after night.
Heavens above,
Gardening in Eden?
It would be bliss
After this.

        Catherine Benson

The Experts

Give three cheers for experts,
They know a thing or two,
And if we didn't have 'em
Whatever would we do?

They built a ship that couldn't sink;
It sailed across the sea.
Its name was the *Titanic*
It's gone down in history.

For years and years the experts knew
The Sun went round the Earth,
And when Copernicus said: 'Wrong!'
They couldn't hide their mirth.

They told Columbus not to sail
Because he might fall off.
They had King Louis bled to death,
Because he'd got a cough.

Lord Kelvin was a scientist –
A *really* clever guy,
Who proved by mathematics
That man would *never* fly.

And now we've all got nuclear power
So give three mighty cheers –
The experts say it can't go wrong
Once in ten thousand years!

Terry Jones

SCAMS AND SCRAPES AND SCANDALS IN SCHOOL

The Painting Lesson

'What's THAT, dear?'
Asked the new teacher.
'It's Mummy,'
I replied.
'But mums aren't green and orange!
You really haven't TRIED.
You don't just paint in SPLODGES;
You're old enough to know
You need to THINK before you work.
Now – have another go.'

She helped me draw two arms and legs,
A face with sickly smile,
A rounded body, dark brown hair,
A hat – and in a while
She stood back, with her face bright pink:
'That's SO much better, don't you think?'

But she turned white
At ten to three
When an orange-green blob
Collected me.

'Hi, Mum!'

Trevor Harvey

Gust Becos I Cud Not Spel

Gust becos I cud not spel
It did not mean I was daft
When the boys in school red my riting
Some of them laffed

But now I am the dictater
They have to rite like me
Utherwise they cannot pas
Ther GCSE

Some of the girls were ok
But those who laffed a lot
Have al bean rownded up
And hav recintly bean shot

The teecher who corrected my speling
As not been shot at al
But four the last fifteen howers
As bean standing up against a wal

He has to stand ther until he can spel
Figgymisgrugifooniyn the rite way
I think he will stand ther for ever
I just inventid it today

Brian Patten

So I'm Proud

Our History teacher says, 'Be proud you're
   Canadians.'
My father says, 'You can be proud you're Jewish.'
My mother says, 'Stand up straight, Kate.
   Be proud you're tall.'

So I'm proud.

But what I want to know is,
When did I have the chance to be
   Norwegian or Buddhist or short?

Jean Little

Season's Greetings

In Art we're always drawing cards
For Hallowe'en or Easter,
Christmas, Harvest Festival,
Each holiday or feast or

Mother's Day or Father's Day,
Any old excuse is
Time to draw *another* card.
I *hate* it – cos I'm useless!

I couldn't draw the Easter chicks
   I couldn't draw their eggs,
I couldn't draw the bunny's ears
   I couldn't draw his legs.

I couldn't draw a harvest sheaf
   I couldn't draw a plough.
I couldn't draw *then* and
   I can't draw now!

Look!

I can't draw robins
   I can't draw snow,
I can't draw holly
   I can't *draw* – no!

I can't draw turkeys
   I can't draw stuffing,
I can't draw Santa Claus
   – I can't draw nuffing!

So *please*, Mrs Stevenson,
Give it a rest!
Don't say, 'It's very nice, and
I can see you've done your best.'

I couldn't give it to my granny,
Or even to my aunt –
Cos I can see it's terrible
Even if *you* can't!

Mick Gowar

The Gerbil's Funeral

The gerbil's going bald, Miss,
The gerbil's lost its hair,
Its neck and face and ears, Miss,
Are practically bare!

Oooh, Miss, what if she dies?
What if, after all,
She's suffering from the plague, Miss?
We could have a funeral!

Who'll bring the coffin?
'I,' said Robin.
'I've got a box that I'm not usin'.
I'll bring the coffin.'

Who'll dig the grave?
'I,' said Dave,
'With my dad's spade,
I'll dig the grave.'

Who'll sing a dirge?
'I,' said Jim,
'I can sing a solemn hymn.
I'll sing a dirge.'

Who'll be chief mourner?
'I,' said Lorna.
'I'm the one who brought her.
I'll be chief mourner.'

Who'll make the cross?
'I,' said Claire.
'I'll carve it with care.
I'll make the cross.'

Who'll bring the flowers?
'I,' said Rose.
   and Daisy
       and Heather . . .

What about me?
What about me?
What about me?

All the boys and the girls
Fell to fighting and to shouting –

WHO'LL BE THE PREACHER?
'I,' said the teacher,
'I'll be the preacher,
If the need arises.
Meanwhile, we'll hope for the best.
Life's full of surprises.
Now, what about this spelling test?'

June Crebbin

Kite

I'm
part of a
project on flight.
I'm supposed to attain
a great height. But
unfortunately
I got stuck
in a tree
so
it
looks
like
I'm
here
for
the
night!

June Crebbin

What Happened to Miss Frugle

Stern Miss Frugle always said
To Peter and his sister
'After school you'll stay behind
If you so much as whisper.'

Then one winter afternoon
While skating on thin ice
The children saw it crack and Miss
Frugle vanish in a trice.

People wondered where she'd gone,
But no one really missed her,
And she was never found because
Peter and his sister

didn't so much as whisper
didn't so much as whisper.

Brian Patten

OODLES OF NOODLES AND LASHINGS OF NOSH

The Battle-hymn of the Ice-cream Connoisseur

Mine eyes have seen the glory of
    Pink Fudge Sundaes
I guzzle 'em on Saturdays and slurp on Mondays
I smuggle 'em to Chapel in my Grandma's undies
As my stomach rumbles on.

Adrian Mitchell

A Cold Snack

A polar bear, fed up with fish,
Decided to eat flowers,
And searched across the snowy wastes
For hours and hours and hours,

Until at last he found a snowdrop
Growing through the ice,
A pretty flower but, thought the bear,
Just right for lunch, just nice.

He curled his paw to snatch it up,
Then stopped . . . Was that a squeak?
And nosing close he saw the snowdrop
Nod and start to speak:

'Oh, Mr Bear, I know I'm small
And you are like a hill,
But if you take one bite of me
I'm sure to make you ill,

'Your fur will turn all greeny-grey,
Loud clangs will fill your head,
And when you try to walk your feet
Will feel like lumps of lead.

'You won't know north from east or west,
You won't know left from right,
And awful dreams of kangaroos
Will wake you up at night.'

The bear stepped back and rubbed a paw
Across his worried face,
Then grunted, turned and loped away
To find his fishing place;

While all around the blizzard wailed
And cruel winds loudly blew,
So no one in the whole, white world
Could hear the snowdrop's: 'Phew!'

Richard Edwards

Peas and Cues

There's a little shop in Kew
Selling multicoloured peas
I use some in my stews
The remaining few I freeze

A chopstick for a cue
Then down upon my knees
Play snooker when I choose
And pot the peas with ease.

Roger McGough

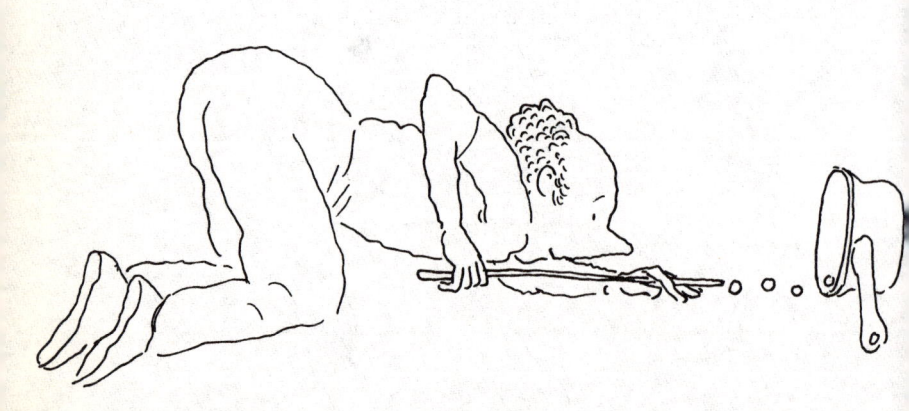

Auntie Meg's Cookery Book

Tom liked his Auntie Meg a lot,
    But even he confessed
She could not cook at all although
    She *thought* she was the best.

She was a sport. She did not pry
    Or lecture Tom or nag;
He loved to go and stay with her
    Except for that big snag:

She was the worst cook in the world
    And *thought* she was the best;
When she spent hours preparing cakes
    He had to act impressed.

But worse, he had to *eat* the things;
    Her rock cakes were no joke;
Not quite as hard as rock perhaps,
    More like well-seasoned oak.

She often made a dumpling stew.
    Today, Tom still recalls
Those dreaded objects in the pot
    Like little cannonballs.

Her rice was gritty, porridge burnt;
   You could have used her steak
For soling shoes, and one dropped bun
   Once made the whole house shake.

The only way to dodge those meals
   Was find some other craze
So interesting it would take up
   All of her waking days.

So Tom persuaded her to write
   A book. 'What kind?' she said.
'About what most appeals to you,
   Pleasing heart and head.'

'A cookery book!' she cried. 'Oh yes!'
　　As lively as a kitten.
'Dear Tom, I'll write the very best
　　That anyone has written.'

And that's exactly what she did,
　　Scribbling day and night.
They had their meals in restaurants
　　To Tom's concealed delight.

At last her masterpiece appeared,
　　And she at once became
An expert in the cooking arts
　　With quickly spreading fame.

A star of radio and screen
　　Was dear old Auntie Meg,
And only Tom, her nephew, knew
　　She couldn't boil an egg.

Vernon Scannell

Giving Potatoes

STRONG MAN: Mashed potatoes cannot hurt you, darling
Mashed potatoes mean no harm
I have brought you mashed potatoes
From my mashed potato farm.

LADY: Take away your mashed potatoes
Leave them in the desert to dry
Take away your mashed potatoes –
You look like shepherd's pie.

BRASH MAN: A packet of chips, a packet of chips,
Wrapped in the *Daily Mail*,
Golden and juicy and fried for a week
In the blubber of the Great White Whale.

LADY: Take away your fried potatoes
Use them to clean your ears
You can eat your fried potatoes
With Birds Eye frozen tears.

OLD MAN: I have borne this baked potato
O'er the Generation Gap,
Pray accept this baked potato
Let me lay it in your heated lap.

LADY: Take away your baked potato
In your fusty musty van
Take away your baked potato
You potato-skinned old man.

FRENCHMAN: She rejected all potatoes
For a thousand night and days
Till a Frenchman wooed and won her
With *pommes de terre Lyonnaises*.

LADY: Oh my corrugated lover
So creamy and so brown
Let us fly across to Lyons
And lay our tubers down.

Adrian Mitchell

Garbage Delight

Now, I'm not the one
To say No to a bun,
And I always can manage some jelly;
If someone gurgles,
'Please eat my hamburgles,'
I try to make room in my belly.
I seem, if they scream,
Not to gag on ice-cream,
And with fudge I can choke down my fright;
But none is enticing
Or even worth slicing,
Compared with Garbage Delight.

    With a nip and a nibble
    A drip and a dribble
    A dollop, a walloping bite:
    If you want to see grins
    All the way to my shins,
    Then give me some Garbage Delight!

I'm handy with candy.
I star with a bar.
And I'm known for my butterscotch burp;
I can stare in the eyes
Of a Toffee Surprise
And polish it off with one slurp.
My lick is the longest,
My chomp is the champ

And everyone envies my bite;
But my talents were wasted
Until I had tasted
The wonders of Garbage Delight.

   With a nip and a nibble
   A drip and a dribble
   A dollop, a walloping bite:
   If you want to see grins
   All the way to my shins,
   Then give me some Garbage Delight,
     Right now!
   Please pass me the Garbage Delight.

Dennis Lee

Things Have Changed

Oy skinny!
she used to say,
make me a sandwich.
Ah, but things have changed now.
Oy fatty!
she says,
make me a sandwich.

Martin Doyle

Seasickness

On a stormy Bass Strait crossing –
People heaving, ferry tossing –
One poor tourist, sick and wailing,
Clutched the rolling midnight railing
When his friend, a real poltroon,
Said, 'Are you waiting for the moon
To come up now?' To which he answered, 'Hell,
Don't say I've swallowed that as well.'

Colin Thiele

Dinner-time Rhyme

Can you tell me, if you please,
Who it is likes mushy peas?
    Louise likes peas.
How about Sam?
    Sam likes spam.
How about Vince?
    Vince likes mince.
How about Kelly?
    Kelly likes jelly.
How about Trish?
    Trish likes fish.
How about Pips?
    Pips likes chips.
How about Pete?
    Pete likes meat.
How about Sue?
    Sue likes stew.
How about Greg?
    Greg likes egg.
How about Pam?
    Pam likes lamb.

OK, then, tell me, if you can –
How about Katerina Wilhelmina Theodora Dobson?

    She goes home for dinner . . .

June Crebbin

Don't Leave the Spoon in the Syrup

The lid was off,
the spoon was in,
the syrup smelled deliciously;
I looked,
I watched,
I sniffed,
and then –
I licked it syrupticiously!

N. Bodecker

Official Notice

Persons with Dogs or Chimpanzees:
Try to distract their attention, please,
When promenading past the Giant Cheese.

Adrian Mitchell

OF MISFITS AND MISFORTUNES

More Work for the Undertaker

Listen to the song I'm going to sing you –
You'll laugh till you haven't any breath –
People as a rule seem to think it funny
When they hear of a violent death.
Poor little Solomon Snoozer,
He behaved like an ass –
He searched round the house with a candle t'other night,
To find a big escape of gas.
    More work for the undertaker,
    Another little job for the tombstonemaker,
    At the local cemetery they've
    Been very very busy on a brand-new grave –
    Snoozer's snuffed it!

Billy Buck by nature was a moocher,
Hard work didn't suit him, it appears –
He had never done one single bit of 'graft'
For nine and thirty years;
Lately he had a bad nightmare,
Bill at once got the knock,
He dreamt he had been out looking for a job –
He couldn't stand the terrible shock.
    More work for the undertaker,
    Another little job for the tombstonemaker,
    At the local cemetery they've
    Been very very busy on a brand-new grave –
    Billiam's blew'd it!

Sammy Shunter laboured on a railway –
His work he was very clever at –
Sam, the other day, was polishing the metals
With a lump of mouldy fat.
Up came a runaway engine,
Sam stood upon the track:
He held up his hand, for he thoroughly believed
He could push the locomotive back.
    More work for the undertaker,
    Another little job for the tombstonemaker,
    At the local cemetery they've
    Been very very busy on a brand-new grave –
    Shunter's shunted!

Peter Piper visited a circus,
He saw what he never could forget –
One of the performers jumped from the ceiling
Of the house into a net.
Peter a day or two after,
Tried a similar drop –
He leapt from a housetop fifty-seven feet,
And fell upon a great big 'slop'!*
    More work for the undertaker,
    Another little job for the tombstonemaker,
    At the local cemetery they've
    Been very very busy on a brand-new grave –
    For Peter and the p'liceman!

* Cop

Little Freddie Figgleton the fat boy,
Last week called upon his uncle Brown;
Just before he left, young Freddie was presented
With a bright new half a crown.
Then, as he felt a bit thirsty,
He went into a shop –
Drank ten lemonades, a dozen ginger beers,
And then there was a great big pop!
    More work for the undertaker,
    Another little job for the tombstonemaker,
    At the local cemetery they've
    Been very very busy on a brand-new grave –
    For Frederick's fragments.

Fred. W. Leigh

Someone's Fear

There's something rather odd about you
said my landlady,
but I'm not sure what it is
so I'm doubling your rent.

Martin Doyle

An Evening in November

   'Twas an evening in November,
     As I very well remember,
I was strolling down the street in drunken pride,
     But my knees were all a-flutter,
     So I landed in the gutter,
And a pig came up and lay down by my side.

   Yes, I lay there in the gutter,
     Thinking thoughts I could not utter,
When a colleen passing by did softly say:
     'Ye can tell a man that boozes
     By the company he chooses.'
At that the pig got up and walked away!

Anon.

The Secret Drawer

'Inside this wardrobe 'ere,' says Des,
'There be one secret drawer
With treasures in, all tucked away
Behind one secret door.
To find that door,' says Des, 'you turns
One knob thing to the side,
To find that knob you got to shift
One hidden, secret slide,
To find that slide you got to raise
One secret, wooden flap,
To find that flap,' says Des, 'you reads
Instructions off a map.
And that's what's got me foxed,' says Des,
'And what I'm frettin' for:
I've gone and left that map inside
The blinkin' secret drawer!'

Richard Edwards

Wobble-dee-woo

What would you do
With a Wobble-dee-woo?
Would you eat it
Or wear it
Or play it?
What would you do
With a Wobble-dee-woo?
(I've only just learned
How to say it.)

What would you do
With a Wobble-dee-woo?
Would you wear it
Or play it
Or eat it?
What would you do
With a Wobble-dee-woo?
(I'm sorry, I'll have
To repeat it.)

What would you do
With a Wobble-dee-woo?
Would you play it
Or eat it
Or wear it?
What would you do
With a Wobble-dee-woo?
(It's driving me mad,
I can't bear it!)

Colin West

Cholmondeley*

A cholmond of mine
Named Cholmondeley
Was stung one afternoon
Most horribly
By a bolmondble bee

(Or it might have been a holmondble bee,
Cholmondeley didn't see).

Cholmondeley was pottering happily
In his garden, when he noticed
– 'Burp! Pardon me!' –
His tolmondy was getting rolmondbly.

He thought, 'I'll pick
A ripe, juicy plolmond
From my plolmond tree.
That should do the trick . . .'

When suddenly –
'Aieeeeeeeeeee!'
That dreadful bolmondble bee
(One of the vicious sort)
Flew up the leg of Cholmondeley's shorts

And stung him
On both cheeks of his bolmond!

Poor Cholmondeley –
What agony!
He grabbed his bolmond and
Dropped his plolmond.

A double tragedy:
Poor Cholmondeley lost his plolmond,
And all he got in return was
A nolmond bolmond!

Mick Gowar

* Cholmondeley is pronounced 'chumly'.

Well-wishers

Ding dong bell,
Pussy's in the well,
And four-and-twenty blackbirds
Are rather glad she fell.

Angela Sidey

Trying to Thank the Begonia

'Big on yer,
Begonia!'
'Begone, yer
Big Oaf!'

Daisy Cheyne

The Cat and the Pig

Once, when I wasn't very big
I made a song about a pig
    Who ate a fig
    And wore a wig
And nimbly danced the Irish jig.

And when I was as small as THAT
I made a verse about a cat
    Who ate a rat
    And wore a hat
And sat (you've guessed) upon the mat.

    And that, I thought, was that.

But yesterday upon my door
I heard a knock; I looked and saw
    A hatted cat
    A wiggèd pig
    Who chewed a rat
    Who danced the jig
    On my doormat!

They looked at me with faces wise
Out of their bright inquiring eyes,
'May we come in? For we are yours,
Pray do not leave us out of doors.
We are the children of your mind
Let us come in. Be kind. Be kind.'

So now upon my fireside mat
There lies a tireless pussy cat
Who all day long chews on a rat
        And wears a hat.
And round him like a whirligig
Dancing a frantic Irish jig
Munching a fig, cavorts a big
        Wig-headed pig.

They eat my cakes and drink my tea.
There's hardly anything for me!
And yet I cannot throw them out
For they are mine without a doubt.

But when I'm at my desk tonight
I'll be more careful what I write.

I'll be more careful what I write.

Gerard Benson

There Was a Young Lady of Spain

There was a young lady of Spain,
Who was terribly sick in a train,
    Not once, but again,
    And again and again,
And again, and again . . . AND AGAIN.

                        Anon.

The Lord Said Unto Moses

The Lord said unto Moses:
'Come forth.'
But he slipped on a banana skin
And came fifth.

Anon.

All's Well That Ends

Peter was awake as soon as daylight sidled into his bedroom. Saturday at last. He jumped out of bed and flung open the curtains. Thank goodness, he thought, not a cloud in the sky. As he gazed out of the window, he wondered about the day ahead. Would his school team win the county cricket trophy? (*No* .) Would he score his first century? (*No, l.b.w. second ball* .) Would Helen be at the party in the evening? (*Yes*.) Would she let him dance with her, walk her home and kiss her? (*No, she'd spend all night smooching and snogging with O'Leary* .) Would the police discover Grandma's body behind the woodshed? (*Yes, on Monday*.) And if so, would they think it was an accident? (*No, sorry*.) Or suicide? (*Hardly*.) Would he be incarcerated? (*What's that?*) Put in prison. (*Yes*.)

But during his time inside, wouldn't he determine to make amends, study hard and gain early parole? Wouldn't he find a steady job and settle down? One day meet a decent girl and raise a family? Eventually, wouldn't he own a national chain of DIY supermarkets, give money to charity, become a model citizen respected and loved by the whole community?
Say yes. (*No*.)
But surely all's well that ends? (*Well* ...)

Roger McGough

Success at Last

Here in this vault lies Ffitch-Wren Ffitch-Wren,
Who did everything over and over again.
He took three or four baths in an average day
And shaved so often his chin wore away,
While the only meals that ever he tasted
Where three good breakfasts – lunch and dinner were wasted!
When he came to marry, he did it by fives,
And was five times divorced from his five wives,
Leaving five sons behind him: Ffitch-Wren, and again,
Ffitch-Wren and Ffitch-Wren and Ffitch-Wren and Ffitch-Wren.
He stumbled and st-stammered and was thought a great dunce –
But success came at last, and he died only once!

Raymond Wilson

QUERIES AND THEORIES

We All Know That Bicycle

We all know that bicycle
Shortens to bike
So why is an icicle
Never an ike?

Marianne Chipperfield

A Query

Oh, cabbage, oh, potato, both sizzling in one pan,
Please settle a dispute for me as quickly as you can,
I'm sorry to inquire, but it has caused me so much trouble:
Which one of you goes 'squeak, squeak, squeak,' and which goes 'bubble, bubble'?

Richard Edwards

A Wasp on a Nettle Said: 'Coo!'

A wasp on a nettle said: 'Coo!
We're in a right mess, me and you.
    We have got to sort out
    What this is about.
Please tell me – who's got to sting who?'

Frank Richards

Logic

A girl said:
'I wrote myself a letter.'
So I said:
'What did it say?'
She said:
'I don't know.
I won't get it till tomorrow.'

A boy said:
'I'm really glad my mum called me Jack.'
I said:
'Why's that?'
He said:
'Because all the kids at school
call me that.'

Michael Rosen

Toe-tally

When I was born I was so small
I had no room for toes at all

But by the time I'd aged a year
My first toes started to appear

And by the time that I was two
You could have counted quite a few.

When I was three and three foot high
My toes began to multiply . . .

And now I've reached the age of four
I'll have to grow a whole foot more!

Charles Wright

Why Did the Children

'Why did the children
put beans in their ears
when the one thing we told the children
they must not do
was put beans in their ears?'

'Why did the children
pour molasses on the cat
when the one thing we told the children
they must not do
was pour molasses on the cat?'

Carl Sandburg

Glasses

Glasses sit snugly, semi-detached
Astride many different noses.
I'd like to know where Superman's go
The moment he metamorphoses.

Exotic as tropical parrots
They perch, or sit tight as pince-nez.
The round ones are miniature portholes
Or 'little moons' as the French say.

They look best when worn as tiaras
Afloat on the waves of your hair
Or hung on a chain at your bosom;
Of course, you can't see with them there

But the biggest advantage of glasses
Has nothing to do with your eyes
For people who wear them can never
Be said to have told bare-faced lies.

Sue Cowling

He's on About a Parrot Now

I sometimes think to myself,
I think . . .
thank goodness
I don't own a parrot
I'd only imitate it all day.

       Martin Doyle

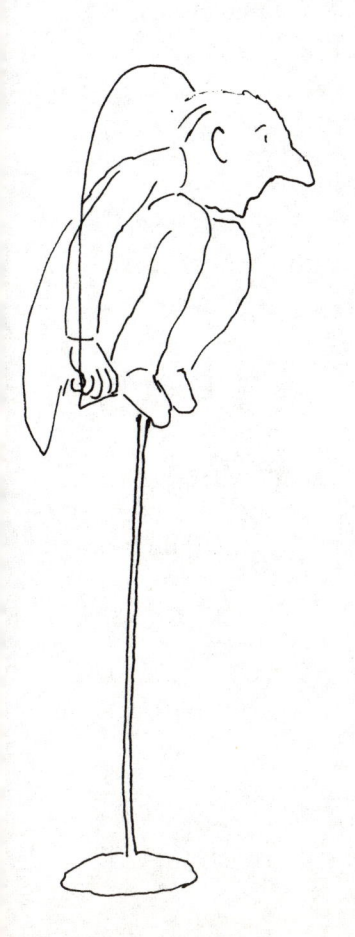

'Which Way to the Post Office, Boy?'

'Which way to the post office, boy?'
  'I don't know.' 'You don't know much, do you?' 'No, but I ain't lost.'

Carl Sandburg

Index of Authors

John Agard	16
Finola Akister	29, 88
Patrick Barrington	13, 67
Catherine Benson	92
Gerard Benson	76, 82, 137
Valerie Bloom	38
N. Bodecker	28, 124
Janeen Brian	80
Daisy Cheyne	136
Marianne Chipperfield	145
Michael Comyns	90
Sue Cowling	150
June Crebbin	21, 104, 106, 123
Jonathan Croall	84
Diane Dawber	39
Roland de Vere, Lord Tryermane	47
Martin Doyle	56, 57, 122, 130, 151
Michael Dugan	87
Richard Edwards	40, 69, 112, 131, 146
Max Fatchen	20, 81
Michael Flanders	18, 30
Roy Fuller	63
Audrey Gorle	77
Mick Gowar	102, 134
Harry Graham	72
Trevor Harvey	99
Adrian Henri	16
Sidney Hoddes	57

Terry Jones   24, 94

Robin Klein   19
Karla Kuskin   78

Dennis Lee   120
Fred W. Leigh   127
Jean Little   101

Mary Macdonald   28
Roger McGough   62, 70, 114, 140
Spike Milligan   86
Lesley Miranda   54
Adrian Mitchell   79, 111, 118, 124
John Mole   60

Mairaed O'Grady   23

Brian Patten   100, 107

Frank Richards   146
Michael Rosen   35, 73, 147
Willy Russell   42

Carl Sandburg   89, 149, 152
Vernon Scannell   52, 115
Angela Sidey   136
Matthew Sweeney   58

Colin Thiele   32, 122

Colin West   37, 55, 87, 132
Raymond Wilson   22, 141
Charles Wright   41, 148

Index of First Lines

A bold Hippopotamus was standing one day	30
A Brother, when asked by the Prior	74
A cholmond of mine	134
A girl said	147
A man went to an antique shop	86
A mosquito	28
A polar bear, fed up with fish	112
A potato clock, a potato clock	70
A wasp on a nettle said: 'Coo!	146
A window-cleaner in our street	72
A year ago last Thursday I was strolling in the zoo	18
As I sat down one evening	50
Ben's done something really bad	37
'Big on yer	136
Call alligator long-mouth	16
Can you tell me, if you please	123
Ding dong bell	136
Do not jump on ancient uncles	78
From where I stood	84
Garden of Eden?	92
Give three cheers for experts	94
Glasses sit snugly, semi-detached	150
Goodbye to my blanket	60
Great	56
Gust becos I cud not spel	100
He hit me on the face, Mummy	54

Here in this vault lies Ffitch-Wren Ffitch-Wren	141
Hickory, dickory, dock	29
I beavered away all the morning	88
I had a haddock	13
I have a pet oyster called Rover	16
I once thought a lot of a friend	56
I saw a silver mermaid with green and purple hair	38
I sometimes think I'd rather crow	26
I sometimes think to myself	151
I was worrying over some homework	40
I wish I was our Sammy	42
I'm	106
If I ever had to choose between you	57
If I were Chief of all Spacemen	80
If only I hadn't had sisters	54
In an old French town	89
In Art we're always drawing cards	102
'Inside this wardrobe 'ere,' says Des	131
Intercede for us dear saint we beseech thee	62
It was dark as I strolled down a country lane	22
Just when I am conducting	81
Ladies and gentlemen	9
Listen to the song I'm going to sing you –	127
Mashed potatoes cannot hurt you, darling	118
Mine eyes have seen the glory of	111
Moby Duck was the terror of the river	24
Mr Lott's allotment	87
Mr Miss	64
My dear Mungo	58
My dog is such a gentle soul	20
My ♡ 🐖 4 U	47

Nibbler, our gerbil, died today	23
Now, I'm not the one	120
Oh, cabbage, oh, potato, both sizzling in one pan	146
Old uncle Samuel, felling trees	87
On a stormy Bass Strait crossing	122
On the coast of Timbuctoo	90
Once, when I wasn't very big	137
One, two, three, four, five –	19
Our History teacher says, 'Be proud you're Canadians.'	101
Our neighbour, Mrs Tuckett	77
Oy skinny!	122
Persons with Dogs or Chimpanzees	124
Peter was awake as soon as daylight sidled into	140
Pussy cat, pussy cat, where have you been?	28
Raising frogs for profit	68
Remarked a young fellow called Hammer	49
Stern Miss Frugle always said	107
Strong man: Mashed potatoes cannot hurt you, darling	118
The fabulous Wizard of Oz	70
The gerbil's going bald, Miss	104
The lid was off	124
The Lord said unto Moses	139
The tree down the street	39
The unicorn had one big horn	29
The world's most enigmatic smile	32
There once was a bard of Hong Kong	76
There was a girl who threw bananas about	79
There was a young bard of Japan	75
There was a young fellow called Tate	49
There was a young lady of Spain	139
There's a little shop in Kew	114

There's something rather odd about you	130
Together down the street they go	55
Tom liked his Auntie Meg a lot	115
'Twas an evening in November	130
Two lovers stood on Sydney bridge	48
We all know that bicycle	145
We sit down to eat	35
What a wonderful bird the frog are	27
What would you do	132
'What's THAT, dear?'	99
'What's the horriblest thing you've seen?'	63
When I was a lad of twenty	67
When I was born I was so small	148
When I was eighteen years of age	52
When my rabbit	21
When the	82
'Which way to the post office, boy?'	152
'Why did the children	149
With the drier switched to high	41
Yesterday I thought I was someone	57
You are so low that, if there was a car on a bridge	48
You can play with dice	73
'You find a sheltered spot that faces south . . .'	69

Acknowledgements

The editor and publishers gratefully acknowledge permission to reproduce copyright poems in this book:

By kind permission of John Agard, c/o Caroline Sheldon Literary Agency 'Don't Call Alligator Long-Mouth Till You Cross River' from *Say It Again, Granny!* published by The Bodley Head, 1986; 'I Beavered Away All the Morning' and 'The Unicorn' by Finola Akister reprinted from *Before You Go to Bed* (Viking Kestrel, 1989), copyright © Finola Akister, 1989, by permission of Penguin Books Ltd; 'Vacancies in Eden or (Wanted: two gardners m/f)' by Catherine Benson, copyright © Catherine Benson, 1990; 'The Cat and the Pig' by Gerard Benson reprinted from *The Magnificent Callisto* (Blackie Children's Books, 1992), copyright © Gerard Benson, 1992, by permission of Penguin Books Ltd, 'The Entry of the Leprechauny Man into Drumloon' reprinted from *Barrow Poems*, a Barrow Poets publication, 1976, copyright © Gerard Benson, 1976 and 'Lim' reprinted from *How to Be Well-versed in Poetry* (Viking Kestrel, 1990), copyright © Gerard Benson, 1990; 'Tall Tales' by Valerie Bloom, copyright © Valerie Bloom, 1989; 'Mosquito' and 'Don't Leave the Spoon in the Syrup' by N. Bodecker reprinted from *Snowman Sniffles and Other Verses* by permission of Faber and Faber Ltd; 'Down-hearted' by Janeen Brian reprinted from *Off the Planet* (Omnibus Books in association with Penguin Books Australia Ltd, 1989), copyright © Janeen Brian, 1989; 'We All Know That Bicycle' by Marianne Chipperfield, copyright © Marianne Chipperfield; 'The McGoos' by Michael Comyns reprinted from *The Trouble With Marrows* (Children's Poolbeg, 1990), copyright © Michael Comyns, 1990; 'Glasses' by Sue Cowling first published by Faber and Faber Ltd, 1991, copyright © Sue Cowling, 1991; 'Dinner-time Rhyme', 'My Rabbit', 'Kite' and 'The Gerbil's Funeral' by June Crebbin reprinted from *The Jungle Sale* (Viking Kestrel, 1988), copyright © June Crebbin, 1988, by permission of Penguin Books Ltd; 'The Tractors' by Jonathan Croall, copyright © Jonathan Croall, 1991; 'Zeroing In' from *Oatmeal Mittens* by Diane Dawber, Borealis Press Ltd, Canada, 1987, copyright © Borealis Press, 1987; 'Someone's Fear', 'Things Have Changed', 'He's on About a Parrot Now', 'Hurrah!' and 'Pain' by Martin Doyle reprinted from *Spine* Journals, November 1991, copyright © Martin Doyle, 1991; 'Improvement' by Michael Dugan reprinted from *Flocks, Socks and Other Shocks* (Penguin Books Australia Ltd, 1987), copyright © Michael Dugan, 1987; 'Lost and Found' and 'A Query' by Richard Edwards reprinted from *A Mouse in My Roof*, published by Orchard Books, London, 1988 and 'The Secret Drawer', 'A Cold Snack' and 'The Wizard Said:' by Richard Edwards reprinted from *Whispers From a Wardrobe* (The Lutterworth Press, 1987), copyright © The Lutterworth Press, 1987, by permission of The Lutterworth Press; 'Control Calling' by Max Fatchen reprinted from *Off the Planet* (Omnibus Books in association with Penguin Books Australia Ltd, 1990), copyright © Max Fatchen, 1990, 'My Dog' by Max Fatchen reprinted from *Fractured Fairy Tales and Ruptured Rhymes* (Omnibus Books in association with Penguin Books Australia Ltd, 1990) copyright © Max Fatchen, 1990; 'Horrible Things' by Roy Fuller reprinted from *The World Through the Window* (Blackie Children's Books, 1989), copyright © Roy Fuller, 1989, by permission of Penguin Books Ltd; 'Shopping' by Audrey Gorle, copyright © Audrey Gorle; 'Season's Greetings' and 'Cholmondeley' by Mick Gowar reprinted from *Third Time Lucky* (Viking Kestrel, 1988), copyright © Mick Gowar, 1988, by permission of Penguin Books Ltd; 'The Painting Lesson' by Trevor Harvey first published by Usborne Books, 1990, copyright © Trevor Harvey, 1990; 'Rover' by Adrian Henri reprinted from *Rhinestone Rhino* (Methuen Children's Books Ltd, 1989), reproduced by permission of Rogers, Coleridge and White Ltd; 'Mashed Potato/Love Poem' by Sidney Hoddes reprinted from *Menu* (Windows Press, 1985), copyright © Sidney Hoddes, 1985; 'The Experts' and 'Moby Duck' reprinted from *The Curse of the Vampire's Socks* by Terry Jones, published by Pavilion Books; 'Fish Fingers' by Robin Klein reprinted from *Fractured Fairy Tales and Ruptured*

Rhymes (Omnibus Books in association with Penguin Books Australia Ltd, 1990), copyright © Robin Klein, 1990; 'Rules' from *Dogs and Dragons, Trees and Dreams* by Karla Kuskin, copyright © 1980 by Karla Kuskin. Selection reprinted by permission of HarperCollins Publishers; 'Garbage Delight' copyright © 1977 Dennis Lee; 'So I'm Proud' from *Hey World, Here I Am!* by Jean Little, text copyright © 1986 Jean Little, selection reprinted by permission of HarperCollins Publishers; 'Up in the Air' by Mary Macdonald reprinted from *Fractured Fairy Tales and Ruptured Rhymes* (Omnibus Books in association with Penguin Books Australia Ltd, 1990), copyright © Mary Macdonald, 1990; 'Peas and Cues' and 'Prayer to Saint Grobianus' by Roger McGough reprinted from *Nailing the Shadow* (Viking Kestrel, 1987) reprinted by permission of the Peters, Fraser & Dunlop Group Ltd, 'All's Well That Ends' and 'Potato Clock' by Roger McGough, copyright © Roger McGough, reprinted by permission of the Peters, Fraser & Dunlop Group Ltd; 'The Eye' by Spike Milligan by permission of Spike Milligan Productions Ltd, copyright © Spike Milligan; 'Don't Hit Your Sister' by Lesley Miranda reprinted from *Black Poetry* (Blackie Children's Books, 1988), copyright © Lesley Miranda, 1988, by permission of Penguin Books Ltd; 'Giving Potatoes' from *All My Own Stuff* by Adrian Mitchell, published by Simon and Schuster. With permission of the Peters, Fraser & Dunlop Group Ltd. 'None of Adrian Mitchell's poems are to be used in connection with any examination whatsoever'; 'The Battle-hymn of the Ice-cream Connoisseur', 'Bebe Belinda and Carl Columbus' and 'Official Notice' from *Nothingmas Day*, published by Allison and Busby Ltd (1984). With permission of the Peters, Fraser & Dunlop Group Ltd. 'None of Adrian Mitchell's poems are to be used in connection with any examination whatsoever.'; 'Goodbye' by John Mole reprinted from *Boo to a Goose* (Peterloo Poets, 1987), copyright © John Mole, 1987, by permission of Peterloo Poets; 'Nibbler' by Mairaed O'Grady, copyright © Margaret Postlethwaite, 1992; 'Gust Becos I Cud Not Spel' and 'What Happened to Miss Frugle' by Brian Patten reprinted from *Gargling With Jelly* (Viking Kestrel, 1985), copyright © Brian Patten, 1985, by permission of Penguin Books Ltd; 'A Wasp on a Nettle Said "Coo!"' by Frank Richards first published by Armarda Books, 1978, copyright © Frank Richards, 1978; 'Hot Food', 'Playing With Words' and 'Logic' by Michael Rosen reprinted from *The Hypnotiser* (André Deutsch Children's Books, 1988), copyright © Scholastic Publications Ltd, 1988; 'Sammy' from *Bloodbrothers* by Willy Russell published by Samuel French Ltd, copyright © Timeact Ltd (lyrics), 1983, copyright © Willy Russell (book), 1985. 'All rights whatsoever in this play are strictly reserved and application for performance, etc., should be made before rehearsal to Casarotto Ramsay Ltd, National House, 60–66 Wardour Street, London W1V 3HP. No performance may be given unless a licence has been obtained.'; 'Why Did the Children' from *The People, Yes* by Carl Sandburg, copyright © 1936 by Harcourt Brace Jovanovich, Inc. and renewed 1964 by Carl Sandburg, reprinted by permission of the publisher; 'The Girl I Did Not Marry' and 'Auntie Meg's Cookery Book' by Vernon Scannell reprinted from *The Clever Potato* (Hutchinson Books Ltd), copyright © Vernon Scannell; 'My Dear Mungo' by Matthew Sweeney first appeared in *The Flying Spring Onion* (Faber and Faber Ltd, 1992), copyright © Matthew Sweeney, 1992; 'Missing Persons' and 'Seasickness' by Colin Thiele reprinted from *Poems in My Luggage* (Omnibus Books in association with Penguin Books Australia Ltd, 1989), copyright © Colin Thiele 1989; 'Wobble-dee-woo', 'Mr Lott's Allottment', 'Miss Murgatroyd' and 'Ben' by Colin West reprinted from *What Would You Do With a Wobble-dee-woo?* (Hutchinson Books Ltd), copyright © Colin West by permission of Random Century Ltd; 'From the Horse's Mouth' and 'Success At Last' by Raymond Wilson reprinted from *To Be a Ghost* (Viking Kestrel, 1991), copyright © Raymond Wilson, 1991, by permission of Penguin Books Ltd; 'Toe-tally' and 'With the Drier Switched to High' by Charles Wright, copyright © Charles Wright.

Every effort has been made to trace copyright holders, but in a few cases this has proved impossible. The editor and publishers apologize for these unwilling cases of copyright transgression and would like to hear from any copyright holders not acknowledged.